THE ULTIMATE
NEW WORLD ORDER

THE ULTIMATE NEW WORLD ORDER

Peace On Earth Good Will Toward Men

David H. Thompson

THE KINGDOMS OF THIS WORLD ARE BECOME THE KINGDOMS OF OUR LORD, AND OF HIS CHRIST; AND HE SHALL REIGN FOREVER AND EVER.

Copyright © 2012 by David H. Thompson.

Library of Congress Control Number:		2012900998
ISBN:	Hardcover	978-1-4691-5434-3
	Softcover	978-1-4691-5433-6
	Ebook	978-1-4691-5435-0

All rights reserved. No part of this book may be reproduced or transmitted in any form or by any means, electronic or mechanical, including photocopying, recording, or by any information storage and retrieval system, without permission in writing from the copyright owner.

This book was printed in the United States of America.

To order additional copies of this book, contact:
Xlibris Corporation
1-888-795-4274
www.Xlibris.com
Orders@Xlibris.com
109348

Let Us Beat Swords into Plowshares Statue at UN building in New York City

Forward

The Bible teaches that all men are created in the image of God. This truth is indicated three times in Genesis 1:26-27. These verses say,

"And God said, Let us make man in our image, after our likeness: and let them have dominion over the fish of the sea, and over the fowl of the air, and over the cattle, and over all the earth, and over every creeping thing that creepeth upon the earth. So God created man in his [own] image, in the image of God created he him; male and female created he them."

Colossians 1:15 says Jesus Christ is the image of the invisible God.

Moreover, Ephesians 2:10 says we are all God's workmanship created IN Christ Jesus unto good works.

In the early church it was understood as a fundamental truth that all mankind were created in Christ Jesus, who is the image of the invisible God. St. John wrote that Jesus Christ is eternal life that lights every man that comes into this world.

However, this fundamental truth about Jesus Christ has been twisted and distorted in the minds of modern day evangelical fundamentalists who say that only people who have accepted Jesus Christ as personal savior are created in Christ Jesus.

This book challenges this twisting and distorting of God's truth and calls it a doctrine of the devil about which St. Paul warned would come in the latter days. (See 2 Timothy 3:1-9) Jesus never asked people to accept him as personal savior.

This book also sets forth the truth that is proclaimed throughout the Bible that God's kingdom is overoming the kingdoms of this world that are ruled by Satan. This overoming by God's kingdom constitutes the universal cleansing salvation of God's creation after which God's glory will fill the earth.

Contents

What's All This Talk about a Coming New World Order?

During the past fifty years, I have been hearing a lot of talk about how a few masterminds are plotting to take over the world to form a New World Order under the control of the Antichrist.

The Internet abounds with information about such a coming New World Order. Wikipedia, the Internet encyclopedia, says the common theme in conspiracy theories about a coming New World Order is that a secretive power elite with a globalist agenda is conspiring to eventually rule the world through an authoritarian world government that will replace all sovereign nation-states, such as the United States of America.

It is believed by some conspiracy theorists that this elite group of men is clandestinely employing an extensive propaganda delusion that imagines this New World Order to be a culmination of history's progress.

This belief leads to speculation that significant occurrences in politics and finance have been orchestrated by an unduly influential cabal operating through many front organizations such as the Trilateral Commission, the Council on Foreign Relations, the Bilderberg Group, and more secretive groups like the Illuminati, the Freemasonry, the Protocols of Zion, and others.

Numerous historical and current events are seen as planned orchestrations in an ongoing plot to achieve world domination through secret political gatherings and secret decision-making processes.

Some of this New World Order propaganda has been promulgated by fundamentalist Christians who believe it is the fulfillment of end-time prophecy concerning the Antichrist.

For example, in 1991, American televangelist Pat Robertson wrote a best-selling book entitled, *The New World Order*.

This book popularized conspiracy theories about recent American history as a theater in which Wall Street, the Federal Reserve System, the Council on Foreign Relations, the Bilderberg Group, and the Trilateral Commission control the flow of events from behind the scenes, nudging us constantly and covertly in the direction of a world government controlled by the Antichrist.

I am surprised that Pat Robertson would write such a book because, as a Bible teacher, he should know very well that our Lord and Savior, Jesus Christ, spoke only about the kingdom of God coming to earth as the ultimate new world order.

Moreover, according to Jesus Christ and the Bible, there *already* exists an evil world order that controls the world.

Jesus called it the kingdom of hell, and he knew it was ruled by Satan who he also knew had usurped control of God's creation from Adam and Eve in the Garden of Eden.

The Bible very clearly proclaims that Jesus Christ is king of God's kingdom and that the church he founded would take over the kingdom of hell and would replace it with God's kingdom that would last forever and ever. This is the audaciously hopeful and profoundly comforting good news (gospel) of the kingdom of God that Jesus said would be preached throughout the earth in the end-times.

These words of Jesus are written over the entrance to CBN TV studios in Virginia Beach, Virginia. So Pat Robertson should be quite aware that God's kingdom is coming to earth. But his ideas about a coming new world order of the Antichrist are unbiblical imaginations that are not of the knowledge of God.

Moreover, St. John wrote nearly two thousand years ago that many Antichrists had already come to earth even back then (see 1 John 2:18).

The Antichrist mentioned in Revelation 13:18, whose number is 666, has no doubt already come because the events in the book of Revelation were said to be things that must shortly come to pass (see Revelation 1:1). This Antichrist was embodied in either Nero or Domitian who were the emperors of Rome in the first century who persecuted God's servants who followed Jesus Christ.

In the prophecy of Daniel, the empire of Rome has great significance because it is the fourth kingdom in Daniel's prophecy during which time God's kingdom would come to earth.

The kingdom of God did indeed come to earth during the reign of the Roman Empire. It came in the form of Jesus Christ who is king of God's kingdom.

This is evident in what Jesus told Pontius Pilate who was the fifth prefect of the Roman province of Judea from AD 26-36.

Jesus told Pontius Pilate that he was a king but that his kingdom was not of the evil world order that ruled the earth at that time.

Jesus told his apostles that he founded his church upon the direct revelation God gave to St. Peter that he was the Christ, the Son of the living God, and he said the gates of hell would not prevail against his church.

Other scripture, such as Revelation 11:15 and Daniel 7:18, confirm that the Church of Christ (the saints of God) will metaphorically and spiritually storm the gates of hell and replace it with the kingdom of God.

The kingdom of God is in essence spiritual, possessing the spiritual attributes of righteousness, peace, and joy in the Holy Spirit.

In view of this truth, it compels one to believe that the coming and ultimate new world order is not at all an evil empire of the Antichrist, but rather it is the very good and righteous kingdom of God, the kingdom of love and light.

Therefore, the ultimate New World Order will be God's kingdom restored on earth just as Jesus and God's holy prophets have proclaimed.

Satan Usurped Dominion Over Earth That God Gave to Adam and Eve

The book of Genesis records that God had first given dominion over God's creation on earth to Adam and Eve (see Genesis 1:28).

But through deception and cunning, Satan was able to wrest control of God's creation from Adam and Eve when he deceived them into eating the forbidden fruit from the tree of knowledge of good and evil.

As the story goes, Adam and Eve were cast out of the Garden of Eden into a world dominated by Satan's vain and violent kingdom of hell, where the earth brought forth thorns and thistles that made Adam's life-sustaining farming efforts more difficult.

And because of what Satan did in deceiving Adam and Eve, God put enmity between Satan and Adam and Eve and between the seed of Adam and Eve and the serpent's seed such that each seed (or offspring) of Adam and Eve would experience perpetual personal conflict (or jihad) with Satan's seed within each soul that would come from Adam and Eve. This perpetual personal conflict is symbolized in the Bible as Satan's seed bruising the heel of Eve's seed. It is also depicted in Romans 8:20 as the creature, including all mankind, being subjected to vanity unwillingly.

It is a fact of life that every man and woman who ever lived on earth has experienced trouble, turmoil, vanity, and selfishness within his or her own soul, so no further proof is needed to substantiate this truth.

But fortunately, that is not the whole story nor by any means the end of the story.

The rest of the story is that while the creature, including mankind, was subjected to vanity, God also subjected his creation to hope. This hope is symbolized by Eve's seed, which is the DNA of Christ Jesus, bruising the head of Satan's seed. People who understand the Bible know and agree that the metaphorical bruising of the head of Satan's seed was fulfilled on the cross of Calvary when Jesus was crucified. But few, if any, understand that this metaphorical bruising of the head of Satan's seed also takes place within the soul of every human being who was created in the image of God. Those who first overcome Satan within their own souls have the first fruits of the harvest of God (see Romans 8:23).

Jesus Christ, in DNA seed form, *is* the image of God in which all men are conceived and created.

St. Paul wrote that all mankind are God's workmanship, created in Christ Jesus unto good works. But everyone knows that we humans don't always do good works even though we were created to do good works.

Instead we often sin and do evil works.

Indeed the truth of mankind is that sometimes we act like the saintly, sinless children of God that we are, and other times we act like the wicked, sinful children of Satan that we also are.

Every human being, except Jesus Christ, is metaphorically like a spiritually conjoined twin: one does good while the other does evil like the troubled man in Stevenson's age-old novel, *The Strange Case of Dr. Jekyll and Mr. Hyde.*

St. Paul called our sinful self the outward man (or sin) while the God-seed in man he called the inward man that delights in the law of God.

Jesus also knew about this good and evil seed in mankind. He sometimes spoke to the evil seed in man as he did when he called the Pharisees the children of the devil. At one point, he even addressed Satan in his apostle, Peter, saying, "Get thee behind me, Satan."

Jesus called his disciples evil in Luke 11:12, saying, "And you being evil know how to give good gifts unto your children."

At another time, Jesus would not commit to people who believed in his name because of the miracles he did. They wanted to crown him king but he would not permit it because he knew it was not yet Father God's timing for him to be crowned king. Scripture says that Jesus knew all men. And he needed not that any should testify of man for he knew what was in man. In this instance, he knew the devil was in these men trying to get him crowned king before God's time.

But this truth of the dual natures of mankind may be too deep or untoward for many to understand or to even want to understand given cherished doctrines of many that say otherwise.

Fundamentalist Christian doctrine alleges that Adam and Eve died spiritually when they ate the forbidden fruit, and therefore, their seed (or offspring) are born spiritually dead and must therefore be born again of the Holy Spirit before they can be saved. St. Augustine popularized this view in the fourth century.

But the truth is, Adam and Eve died from becoming carnally minded; their spirits could not die because they came from God and are therefore immortal. Romans 8:6 confirms the reality of carnally minded death, saying, "*For to be carnally minded is death but to be spiritually minded is life and peace.*"

The spirits of Adam and Eve came from God and are of God and are therefore immortal and cannot die. Only mankind's physical bodies die and return to the dust of the earth from whence they were made while their spirits return to God who gave them as it says in Ecclesiastes 12:7. The meaning of death is separation. When people died in the Bible, it is said they gave up the ghost (spirit) as was the case with Ananias and Sapphira in the New Testament book of Acts 5.

Death is the separation of the physical body from the spirit. Carnally minded death is the separation of man's thinking from God's thinking.

On the cross, Jesus said to the Father, "Into thy hands I commend my spirit." And his spirit was separated from his body.

Then Father God (a.k.a. the ancient of days) dispatched Jesus's spirit to release all departed spirits held captive in the prison house of death called Hades in the Greek tongue (Sheol in Hebrew). It housed those spirits who were at some time disobedient before the flood of Noah (see 1 Peter 3:19-20). These spirits were all still existing with God, but they had no physical bodies to inhabit. Revelation 6:9 depicts departed spirits of the martyrs under the altar of God in heaven.

But that is off the subject of this book; therefore, I will return to what many people call the real world to further elaborate upon the sound thesis of this book that the ultimate New World Order will be the kingdom of God coming to earth just as Jesus preached.

He even taught us to pray, "Thy kingdom come, thy will be done on earth as it is in heaven . . . for thine is the kingdom and the power and the glory forever. Amen."

Men with spiritually well-developed minds of Christ, like St. Paul's, know that Jesus's work on the cross was just the beginning of his work of salvation to orchestrate the restoration of God's kingdom on earth. On the cross, when Jesus said, "It is finished," he was referring to the finishing of the transgression in the Garden of Eden that would culminate, metaphorically speaking, with the bruising of Satan's head in fulfillment of Genesis 3:15 and Daniel 9:24.

However, the ending of sin and the reconciliation of iniquity, I believe, are distinct and separate events that would follow the event called the finishing of the transgression.

St. John wrote in 1 John 3:8 that Jesus was manifested that he might destroy the works of the devil. I believe this work of Jesus Christ is equivalent with the event called the ending of sin. The work of the devil is metaphorically equivalent with what we call sin. Sin is a disease of the human mind caused by a viral infection just like what happens in a computer that acquires a virus. I believe that in the Bible, the metaphorical equivalents to mind viruses are the fiery darts of Satan. (To understand how viruses of the mind work, read Richard Brodie's book entitled *Virus of the Mind*.)

Jesus went about preaching, "Repent, for the kingdom of God is at hand," as he healed the sick and set the captives free, according to scripture.

Jesus associated the coming of the kingdom of God to earth with the casting out of Satan. He told the Jewish religious leaders, "If I with the finger of God cast out devils, then no doubt the kingdom of God has come upon you."

He also associated the judgment of this world (Satan's kingdom of hell) as synonymous with the casting out of Satan and the removal of his kingdom of hell from earth, saying, "*Now is the judgment of this world. Now is the Prince* [Satan of this world] *cast out. And I, if I be lifted up, I will draw all men unto me*" (see John 12:31-32).

The truth is, when Satan is cast out, the perpetual enmity between Satan and mankind will be ended and nothing will hinder or prevent all mankind from being drawn to Jesus.

This is what the conversion and salvation of mankind is all about. It is universal. It will happen to all mankind and all living creatures, even plants and animals that have been held in the bondage of Satan's corruption for thousands of years.

In summary, the work of Jesus to cast out Satan saves all of God's creation from the corruption of Satan and restores God's kingdom on earth. Amen.

God's Kingdom Is the Ultimate
New World Order

When Jesus walked the earth almost two thousand years ago, he said God's kingdom was at hand at that time. And it was. Jesus does not lie. God's kingdom fully manifested on the day of Pentecost when the 120 people in the upper room were converted by the power of the Holy Spirit to become the sons of God. They were the first fruits of God's harvest of mankind (see Romans 8:23). They were all converted in their hearts and minds to become loving and unselfish. This enabled them to love each other and live together in peace and harmony, sharing all things in common, with no man selfishly considering anything his own. The wealthy among them were moved by the Holy Spirit to voluntarily sell their excess houses and lands. And they deposited the proceeds of the sales at the apostles' feet to be redistributed to those in need. As a result, all needs of this community were met as God's abundant kingdom came upon them.

This occurrence happened again a few days later, and the two events are both recorded in the book of Acts: in Acts 2:41-47 and again in Acts 4:31-37. In the later account, the Holy Spirit again empowers another larger group (numbered in the thousands) of Christ's followers to become the loving and unselfish sons of God so they would join with the first group of 120 souls in love, peace, and harmony, sharing all things in common, with no man selfishly considering anything his own. And again the wealthy sold houses and lands to redistribute their wealth to those in need. And again all needs were met, and the new kingdom community continued to enjoy prosperity, having favor with all the people.

An honest, inquiring mind might think, *Wow! That's great! But what happened to that early kingdom community? Does such a kingdom community still exist on earth today?*

The Times and Seasons of God

In God's plan for earth, there is a time and season for all his purposes to be carried out. Sometimes God does things suddenly while other things he does gradually, all according to his plan and purpose. The coming of God's kingdom is a spiritual event that happens both suddenly and gradually. The coming of the king of God's kingdom, Jesus Christ, came suddenly for those who saw and encountered him. Also the coming of God's kingdom came suddenly upon those who experienced living in the kingdom community of saints shortly after Jesus ascended to heaven.

But for most people, God's kingdom will come gradually like a grain of mustard seed growing in their hearts as they contemplate what God did in Jesus to reconcile himself to the world to bring in everlasting righteousness as prophesied in Daniel 9:24.

As the word of God's kingdom enters into their hearts and minds, they will gradually become the loving, unselfish sons of God who will be looking for God's kingdom community to manifest on earth. When God brings these sons of God together, they will form a kingdom community that will overtake the kingdoms of hell on earth in fulfillment of Revelation 11:15.

The Amish and Mennonite communities of today approximate God's kingdom on earth in many ways, but they are still greatly influenced by the traditions of their mostly German forefathers who were all men who were subjected to vanity and hope like all of us.

The early kingdom community depicted in the book of Acts was not sustained because the vanity of the devil was still at work in people like Ananias and Sapphira. Satan caused them to selfishly withhold some of the proceeds from the sale of their properties. The Holy Spirit revealed this to St. Peter who told them they had lied to the Holy Spirit. As a consequence, they gave up the ghost (spirit) and were removed bodily from what God was doing at that time. This brought the fear of God upon the community. But even so, the spirit of God was eventually quenched when self-oriented, humanist-thinking men entered the early kingdom community and seized control, believing they could orchestrate God's kingdom on their own without God.

But scripture says true: "Except the Lord build the house [the kingdom] those who labor to build it labor in vain" (see Psalm 127:1).

The coming of God's kingdom upon mankind is synonymous with God's salvation (redemption) of his creation from the corruption of Satan.

Romans 8:20-25 addresses this great salvation of God as part of God's perfect will and plan for his creation.

Simply stated in a nutshell, God subjected his creation (including mankind) to vanity without its consent while at the same time he subjected it to hope. This hope is embodied in God's only begotten son who he sent to earth to destroy the works of the devil and to free God's creation from the bondage of corruption of the devil to the glorious liberty of the children of God. For we know that the whole of creation groaneth and travaileth in pain until now. And not only they but ourselves also, who have the first fruits of the spirit. Even we, ourselves, groan within ourselves, waiting for the adoption, to wit, the redemption of our bodies, for we are saved by hope. But hope that is seen is not hope. For what a man sees, why does he hope for it?

But if we hope for what we see not, then do we with patience wait for it?

This hope in which we were all subjected is addressed throughout St. Paul's epistles.

In Colossians 1:27, he addresses the mystery of the indwelling Christ in every man and calls it the hope of glory.

In 1 Corinthians 13:13, he lists *hope* along with *faith* and *charity* as being vital attributes of the children of God.

Because salvation and the kingdom of God are solely the works of God, they are freely given to all mankind with no distinction based upon what a man may think, believe, or do. All mankind are God's children whom he loves, and his master plan does not call for any of his beloved children to be separated from him forever; for a temporary time period for chastening and cleansing, yes. But forever, no!

The Work of Salvation Is Accomplished Only by God through Jesus Christ

God's work of salvation has been a topic of much debate and discussion throughout church history.

Modern-day fundamentalist evangelical churches adamantly teach that a man is saved when, by an act of his will, he accepts Jesus Christ as his personal savior. At that moment, it is believed that man is born again into the family of God.

However, St. John wrote in John 1:13 that being born of God was not effected by the will of man (through belief) nor by the will of the flesh (through good works) nor by bloodline (as the Pharisees believed).

John the Baptist told the Pharisees they could not claim salvation because they had Abraham as their father. John told them God could raise up children of Abraham from the stones.

And Jesus said that salvation was impossible with men, but with God, all things are possible (see Mark 10:27).

The evangelical idea that salvation is a gift of God, like some material gift that must be received, is unbiblical. Actually, the gifts of God—like grace, faith, and our lives—cannot cognitively be refused. When a newborn baby gets a slap on its rear end and begins breathing, its brain is not yet developed enough for it to cognitively refuse to breathe and to thereby refuse its gift of life.

When God breathed his spirit into Adam and Eve, they received God's life, which is immortal and eternal. Their brains were no doubt like a newborn baby's brain and were not cognitively developed enough for them to refuse their gift of eternal life.

The life of every newborn baby is likewise immortal, eternal life. All the spirits of mankind are immortal and eternal because they came from God, and they return to God when a man dies physically. Only their bodies die and return to the dust from whence they were made (see Ecclesiastes 12:7).

Moreover, Jesus always spoke of salvation and the kingdom of God as coming upon us.

Jesus told Zacchaeus, the chief tax collector, that salvation had come to his house. His salvation was evidenced by his changed heart and mind to stop cheating people in his tax-collection work. His changed heart and mind did not bring his salvation. Zacchaeus showed forth works meet for repentance when he stopped cheating people and he gave back fourfold what he had stolen in tax collection.

Zacchaeus's salvation came because Jesus first accepted him and chose him and told him to come down from the sycamore tree because Jesus wanted to abide with him.

In God's salvation, he always chooses and empowers us first, even while we are sinners. In God's salvation, we are empowered to believe God and to do his perfect will. For as we work out our own salvation with fear and trembling, it is God who works in us both to do his will and to do his good pleasure (see Philippians 2:12-13).

It may sound like this verse says that *we are supposed to* work out our own salvation by an act of our will, but if that were the case, then it would contradict Ephesians 2:8-9 that says, "We are saved not of ourselves not of works lest any man should boast."

Moreover, Titus 3:5-6 says, "*Not* by works of righteousness that we have done but according to his mercy he saved us by the washing of regeneration, and renewing of the Holy Spirit."

The washing of regeneration is a work that God does spiritually in us just like the renewing of our minds. Some of the early church fathers mistakenly taught that the washing of regeneration was water baptism that we choose, by an act of our will, to undergo. But the truth is, man has no choice in salvation. It is something that God works out in us regardless of our choice or will to believe or to do good works.

God does *not* wait for man to choose him and then weep if man does not choose him. No, Jesus draws men to him. He does not wait for man to choose him. And when Satan is cast out, there is no power on earth that will tempt mankind to resist the draw of Jesus.

God's sovereign and perfect will and plan is to save all men and bring us all to the knowledge of the truth. He has written his plan in mankind's spiritual DNA, which is the spiritual DNA of Christ.

Therefore, it is just a matter of God's timing when all men will eventually be matured to the fullness of the stature of Jesus Christ as per Romans 8:28-30. In the DNA development process, Christ is born (or formed) in every human soul.

Galatians 4:19 confirms and reiterates this truth where St. Paul says, "*My little children, I travail in birth again until Christ be formed in you.*"

Utopian Movements of Man That Have Quenched the Spirit of God

The New Age Movement

During the socially tumultuous era of the sixties, I heard about the New Age movement and the age of Aquarius. At that time, I did not have much understanding of what it was all about, but I liked the theme song that proclaimed, "This is the dawning of the age of Aquarius." And I also liked the idea—it conveyed of peace and harmony among all people. The New Age movement seems to embody a longing for peace and harmony among all people of the earth who are believed to be brothers and sisters of the family of God. I now realize that the concept of the fatherhood of God and the brotherhood of man comes from the Bible. I used to think it was just a woo-woo New Age concept that had no basis in reality and truth.

As I look back at the sixties, I now realize what may have motivated the social upheaval. Perhaps it was mass dissatisfaction with the corruption and violence in the world that was epitomized by the Vietnam War. In the midst of that dissatisfaction, I believe God placed in the hearts of that younger, so-called hippie generation a desire to seek first God's kingdom and his righteousness. This desire for God's kingdom was reflected in the lyrics of a few songs from that era, such as "Woodstock" and

John Lennon's song, "Imagine," that is clearly a cry for God's kingdom of peace and harmony to come to earth.

But this cry was dampened by such ideologies as found in books by Gary Allen, such as his 1971 book entitled *None Dare Call It Conspiracy* and the 1974 book *Rockefeller: Campaigning for the New World Order*.

Such books warn that the so-called age of Aquarius, the New Age movement, and the coming New World Order are all the works of the devil.

After what seemed to be the fall of communism in the early 1990s, the main demonized scapegoat of the American far right shifted seamlessly from cryptocommunists who plotted on behalf of the imagined red menace to mythical globalists who plot on behalf of the imagined New World Order.

The relatively painless nature of the shift may have been due to growing right-wing populist opposition to corporate internationalism. But also it may have been in part due to the basic underlying apocalyptic belief in the coming new world order of the Antichrist.

In his September 11, 1991, "Toward a New World Order" speech to a joint session of congress, President George H. W. Bush described his objectives for post-Cold War global governance and cooperation with former Soviet states:

> "*Until now, the world we have known has been a world divided—a world of barbed wire and concrete block, conflict and cold war. Now we can see a new world coming into view. A world in which there is a very real prospect of a New World Order. In the words of Winston Churchill, a 'world order' in which the principles of justice and fair play—protect the weak against the strong . . . A world where the United Nations, freed from cold war stalemate, is poised to fulfill the historic vision*

*of its founders. A world in which freedom and respect for
human rights find a home among all nations."*

After the speech, the *New York Times* observed that
progressives were denouncing this new world order as a
rationalization for American imperial ambitions in the Middle
East while conservatives rejected new security arrangements
altogether and fulminated about any possibility of UN revival
and dominance.

When President Bush announced that his new foreign policy
would help build a new world order, his phrasing surged through
the Christian and secular hard right like an electric shock since
the phrase "new world order" had been used to represent the
collectivist one-world government for decades. Some Christians
saw Bush as signaling the end-times betrayal by a world leader.

Secular anticommunists saw a bold attempt to smash US
sovereignty and impose a tyrannical collectivist system run by
the United Nations.

Conspiracy theorists like Pat Robertson think they are doing us
a great service by exposing groups like the Trilateral Commission
and the Council on Foreign Relations whose goals include the
establishment of a one-world government. But there is no indication
in Bible prophecy that a new world order of the Antichrist is still
yet to come as a counterfeit of the kingdom of God.

The counterfeit kingdom has been on earth ever since Adam
and Eve ate from the tree of knowledge.

And the counterfeit kingdom has also slowly grown and
developed like a grain of mustard seed over thousands of years just
like Jesus said the kingdom of God would grow and develop.

But in the later days, according to Bible prophecy, the kingdom
of God will overtake the counterfeit kingdom and be the most
dominant tree in the garden, metaphorically speaking.

Therefore the goal of one-world government will only be
achieved by God's kingdom under God's direction.

The fears of Pat Robertson and other conspiracy theorists of a new world order under control of the Antichrist in the later days are not founded in the knowledge of God that is revealed in scripture.

Such fear and hype quenches the spirit of God, causing God to stand aside to allow mankind to mess things up, leaning toward their own foolish understanding, not trusting God in all things (see Proverbs 3:5-6).

The quenching of the spirit of God does not mean in any way that God's power can be quenched or overcome. God's power cannot be quenched by any power in the universe. All power was given to Jesus Christ, God's Son, who was only begotten by him. But all mankind, except for Jesus, were also begotten of Satan as well as of God.

When God, as a loving father, sees one of his sons taking control of things before God ordains it, then Father God just backs off and lets that son experience operating on his own limited knowledge and understanding until subsequently, through lack of knowledge, that son will fail.

Then when his son fails, our loving, ever merciful heavenly Father returns to help his son pick up the pieces of his life and to direct him to start over in accordance with God's timing and purpose.

It is the nature of immature sons to be impetuous and precocious know-it-alls who let their lustful imaginations run wild so they wind up doing evil. God just laughs.

Everything man attempts to do, leaning toward his own understanding, will always lead to evil, death, and separation from God, but not forever.

God, in his loving mercy, will not let his human children remain separated from him forever.

Eventually, our loving Father will renew our corrupted understanding and even create in us a new heart as King David prayed (see Psalms 51:10 and Ezekiel 36:26-27).

Many Americans who have been led astray by conspiracy theorists like Pat Robertson, especially right-wing conservatives, feel that a coming one-world government would undermine the sovereignty of the United States. Because of this question of sovereignty, some of our conservative leaders are wary of the growing power and influence of the United Nations. They do not want American soldiers coming under the command of the UN.

But is the UN to be feared as an instrument of a sinister conspiracy to establish an evil New World Order? Or could the UN be an instrument of God to establish his kingdom on earth? This is a very important question because how we answer it will determine our policy toward the UN.

There is a sculpture in front of the UN building in New York City that depicts a man beating his sword into a plowshare (see the second page of this book). This sculpture may indicate that the UN is an instrument of God because this sculpture depicts a prophecy of God's kingdom coming to earth when man will learn war no more. Isaiah 2:4 says,

> *"And he shall judge among the nations, and shall rebuke many people: and they shall beat their swords into plowshares, and their spears into pruning hooks: nation shall not lift up sword against nation, neither shall they learn war anymore."*

> But Joel 3:10 says the opposite. It says, *"Beat your plowshares into swords, and your pruning hooks into spears: let the weak say, I am strong."*

So what gives here? Does the Bible contain contradictions so it can't be trusted? Perhaps it all depends upon the proper understanding of the times and purposes of God.

As with all writing, the Bible must be rightly divided and properly interpreted to make sense out of such seeming contradictions.

We must recognize as King Solomon did that from God's viewpoint, there are times and seasons for all of God's purposes under heaven. There is a time to love and a time to hate, a time of war and a time of peace.

Isaiah 2:4 depicts a time of peace when God's purpose is for his kingdom to prevail on earth while Joel 3:10 depicts a time of war preparation during a different time and purpose that involves God's judgment.

Since God renewed my mind about eight years ago, I now understand that the theme of Bible prophecy mysteriously proclaims that the perfect will and purpose of God has always been to establish his righteous kingdom on earth to be ruled by Jesus and his saints. This is reflected in Daniel 7 and in Revelation 19 that depicts Jesus and his saints as a conquering spiritual army riding white horses and dressed in fine linen, coming to earth to finally overthrow the forces of evil so God's spiritual kingdom is restored and established on earth forever in the hearts and minds of all mankind.

Revelation 10:7 depicts the coming of God's kingdom to earth as a mystery that should be finished in the days of the voice of the seventh trumpet. As he hath declared to his servants, the prophets:

> "But in the days of the voice of the seventh angel, when he shall begin to sound, the mystery of God should be finished, as he hath declared to his servants the prophets" (Revelation 10:7).

In Revelation 11:15, God's kingdom is envisioned as supplanting the evil kingdoms of Satan. This also happens at the time the seventh angel sounds his trumpet, so the events depicted in these two verses are the same event that is the coming of the kingdom of God to earth.

> *"And the seventh angel sounded; and there were great voices in heaven, saying, 'The kingdoms of this world are become the kingdoms of our Lord, and of his Christ; and he shall reign forever and ever.'"*

Father God sent his Son, Jesus, to earth to carry out his work of restoring his kingdom on earth.

For the past two thousand years, Jesus has been carrying on this kingdom-restoration work in the hearts and minds of mankind and through the governments of mankind that God has established on earth.

God has been working through many people to carry out his plan. Some may be very aware of how God is using them. Others may not be as aware of his direction in their lives. God may even use people who say they are atheists. And others God calls into his service may be serving as operatives in Satan's kingdom as was the case with Saul of Tarsus during the New Testament times.

I believe that the restoration of God's kingdom on earth is in its final stages of completion.

Therefore I believe God's completed kingdom will be the ultimate new world order that was long ago prophesied and depicted in Isaiah 9:6-7:

> *"For unto us a child is born, unto us a son is given: and the government shall be upon his shoulder: and his name shall be called Wonderful, Counselor, The mighty God, The everlasting Father, The Prince of Peace. Of the increase of his government and peace there shall be no end, upon the throne of David, and upon his kingdom, to order it, and to establish it with judgment and with justice from henceforth, even forever. The zeal of the LORD of hosts will perform this."*

God's Kingdom Came During the Times of the Roman Empire

One of the most astoundingly clear prophecies of God's kingdom coming to earth is found in the seventh chapter of the prophetic book of Daniel.

This prophecy depicts God's kingdom as manifesting on earth during the Roman Empire.

Amazingly, Daniel 7:13-23 prophesies,

> "*I saw in the night visions, and behold, one like the Son of man came with the clouds of heaven to the Ancient of days, and they brought him near before him. And there was given to him dominion, and glory, and a kingdom, that all people, nations, and languages, should serve him: his dominion is an everlasting dominion, which shall not pass away, and his kingdom that which shall not be destroyed . . .*
>
> *I beheld, and the same horn made war with the saints, and prevailed against them; Until the Ancient of days came, and judgment was given to the saints of the most High; and the time came that the saints possessed the kingdom. Thus he said, 'The fourth beast shall be the fourth kingdom upon earth, which shall be diverse from*

all kingdoms, and shall devour the whole earth, and shall tread it down, and break it in pieces.'"

This prophecy tracks well with Isaiah 9:6-7 that was just quoted. The prophecies of Isaiah came to the tribe of Judah over two hundred years before Daniel's prophesies. The prophet Daniel was also a son of the tribe of Judah. Both Daniel and Isaiah prophesied out of the tribe of Judah because, historically, the tribe of Judah held the scepter of God's rule that indicated that the ruler of God's kingdom would come out of the tribe of Judah. Genesis 49:10 says, *"The sceptre shall not depart from Judah, nor a lawgiver from between his feet, until Shiloh come; and unto him shall the gathering of the people be."*

The Empire of Rome was the most far-reaching New World Order of Daniel's prophecy. The first world order of Daniel's prophecy was the kingdom of Babylon under King Nebuchadnezzar. The next world kingdom was Media-Persia, and the third was Greece under Alexander the Great. Alexander conquered Egypt and most of the rest of the middle portion of the inhabited world at that time.

The Roman Empire was the fourth kingdom of Daniel's prophecy. It was said to be diverse from all kingdoms and it would devour the whole earth and tread it down and break it in pieces.

The Roman Empire grew in power and influence as it conquered by sword most of the known world of that time that included Europe and the British Isles. This constituted only about one third of the inhabited earth at that time. The other two thirds of the inhabited world that included the Americas, India, and the Far East were relatively unknown to the Romans but not, of course, unknown to God. God had future plans for the Americas that had not yet been discovered by Europeans. During Rome's conquests, these lands were no doubt too far away from Rome's theater of operations to even be considered for conquest. However, even after history recorded the fall of the Roman Empire in AD 476, the influence of Roman culture and rule of law has continued to expand throughout the world, even into the other two-thirds of the world that include the Americas, India, and the Far East.

From AD 500 to 1806, much of Europe was dominated by a German kingdom that was called the Holy Roman Empire because it was believed to be a continuation of the old Roman Empire under the Roman Catholic Church.

The Roman Catholic Church taught the doctrinal error that the Holy Roman Empire was the kingdom of God on earth that replaced Israel. But as the French philosopher Voltaire wrote, it was neither holy, Roman, or even an empire.

For sure it was not the kingdom of God on earth because it had few attributes of the real kingdom of God. It did not bring everlasting righteousness and peace on earth and goodwill toward men, but it did operate under the rule of law that is an attribute of God's kingdom.

The old Roman Empire conquered by means of armed force and also by means of accommodating the laws, customs, ideas, and beliefs of the nations it conquered for the sake of maintaining peace. Because of this, the government of Rome flowered from 27 BC to AD 180 and was called Pax Romana or *the peace of Roman rule*. (Remember that *peace* is an attribute of the kingdom of God!)

The Empire of Rome seemed always to be in a state of flux and transition as it expanded its influence throughout the world. In some cases, some Romans adopted and amalgamated the laws, ideas, and beliefs of conquered nations to be their own. This may have been the case with the laws, ideas, and beliefs of the conquered nation of Israel that Rome destroyed in AD 70 along with the Jewish Temple.

The Roman centurion named Cornelius that St. Peter visited (see Acts 10) adopted the ways of the Hebrew God. Some Romans also adopted the laws and religious beliefs of ancient Greece. With the so-called Christian Emperor Constantine of the fourth century AD, the ways and means of the Judeo-Christian God may have finally been fully accepted and solidified into the laws of Rome. I don't know if this is true or not, but I do know that the progress of God to establish his kingdom's law and order has been an ongoing, gradual process throughout human history. In many ways, the kingdom of God can be seen as the progress of mankind's civilization to become more righteous, tolerant, and loving under the rule of law.

In the United States, I believe this is evidenced in the legends, lore, and law of the American people. For example, in the legend of Wyatt Earp, the famous lawman of the American Wild West, the theme song of *The Life and Legend of Wyatt Earp* TV series said that Wyatt Earp "cleaned up the country, the old Wild West Country, he made law and order prevail." And don't forget the legend of the famous fictitious superhero called Superman who fought a never-ending battle for truth, justice, and the American way.

I believe such legends and myths reflect the hand of God at work to incorporate his kingdom's law and order into all governments of the world. The royal law of God's kingdom is not complicated. It is very easy to understand. It is simply this: "Thou shalt love thy neighbor as thyself" (see James 2:8).

Jesus, the king of God's kingdom, said that the greatest law was to love the Lord thy God with all your heart, and the second was to love your neighbor as yourself. He said all law hangs upon these two basic laws.

The Bible says God would write his laws on men's hearts (see Jeremiah 31:33).

America's founding fathers understood this, and they wisely built our nation upon these kingdom laws of God. In this way, God has shed his grace upon the United States of America.

World history recorded in the Bible reflects how God incorporated his righteous law into the governments of ancient Egypt and Babylon.

In ancient Egypt, God orchestrated that his servant Joseph would rule as Pharaoh's second-in-command to administer God's righteous and frugal kingdom ways and means to save Egypt and its neighbors from perishing through famine.

And in ancient Babylon, God used his servant Daniel to help teach King Nebuchadnezzar about the reality of God's kingdom's rule on earth.

This truth is reflected in the words of King Nebuchadnezzar himself after God had put him through a time of severe chastening:

> *"And at the end of the days* [of chastening] *I Nebuchadnezzar lifted up mine eyes unto heaven, and mine understanding returned unto me, and I blessed the most High, and I praised and honored him that liveth for ever, whose dominion is an everlasting dominion, and his kingdom is from generation to generation: And all the inhabitants of the earth are reputed as nothing: and he doeth according to his will in the army of heaven, and among the inhabitants of the earth: and none can stay his hand, or say unto him, 'What doest thou?' At the same time my reason returned unto me; and for the glory of my kingdom, mine honour and brightness returned unto me; and my counsellors and my lords sought unto me; and I was established in my kingdom, and excellent majesty was added unto me. Now I Nebuchadnezzar praise and extol and honour the King of heaven, all whose works are truth, and his ways judgment: and those that walk in pride he is able to abase"* (Daniel 4:35-37).

Fast forward to the twentieth century of our Lord; we see that the US dollar depicts an all-seeing eye atop an unfinished pyramid that has the Latin words "novus ordo seclorum" inscribed beneath the pyramid. To the right of the all-seeing eye are the words, "In God We Trust."

Inquiring minds might want to know the meaning of the pyramid and why the words "new order of the ages" are written in Latin, which was the now-defunct language of the old Roman world order. And why are the words "In God We Trust" on the US dollar and other US bills and coins? And why do we refer to the twentieth century as "of our Lord"? Just what gives here?

The answers to these questions will further reveal that the mystery of God's kingdom coming on earth is consistent with the talk of a new world order coming to earth. But God's kingdom will be a good New World Order, not an evil one as the conspiracy theorists say.

From God's perspective, he ordained that the Roman Empire play a major role in his master plan to establish and complete his kingdom on earth. It was during the times of the Roman Empire that God sent his son Jesus to earth to proclaim that God's kingdom was at hand. And indeed God's kingdom was at hand then because Jesus Christ, as king, embodied the fullness of God's kingdom.

Jesus literally stood face-to-face with the mighty Roman Empire that ruled Israel at that time.

This face-to-face encounter of Jesus with the Roman Empire is recorded in chapters 18 and 19 of the Gospel of John.

I have here quoted only portions of these chapters for the sake of brevity. But to fully understand what was going on here with respect to God establishing his new world order on earth, these verses should be read with a spiritually discerning eye for details, paying particular attention to the words of Jesus written in bold.

"Then Pilate entered into the judgment hall again, and called Jesus, and said unto him, 'Art thou the King of the Jews?' Jesus answered him, **'Sayest thou this thing of thyself, or did others tell it thee of me?'** *Pilate answered, 'Am I a Jew? Thine own nation and the chief priests have delivered thee unto me: what hast thou done?' Jesus answered,* **'My kingdom is not of this world: if my kingdom were of this world, then would my servants fight, that I should not be delivered to the Jews: but now is my kingdom not from hence.'** *Pilate therefore said unto him, 'Art thou a king then?' Jesus answered,* **'Thou sayest that I am a king. To this end was I born, and for this cause came I into the world, that I should bear witness unto the truth. Every one that is of the truth heareth my voice.'** *Pilate saith unto him, 'What is truth?' And when he had said this, he went out again unto the Jews, and saith unto them, 'I find in him no fault at all'"* (John 18:33-38).

"The Jews answered him, 'We have a law, and by our law he ought to die, because he made himself the Son of God.' When Pilate therefore heard that saying, he was the more afraid; And went again into the judgment hall, and saith unto Jesus, 'Whence art thou?' **But Jesus gave him no answer.** [This specifically fulfills the prophecy of Isaiah 53:7: *"He was oppressed, and he was afflicted, yet he opened not his mouth: he is brought as a lamb to the slaughter, and as a sheep before her shearers is dumb, so he openeth not his mouth."*] *Then saith Pilate unto him, 'Speakest thou not unto me? Knowest thou not that I have power to crucify thee, and have power to release thee?' Jesus answered,* **'Thou couldest have no power at all against me, except it were given thee from above: therefore he that delivered me unto thee hath**

the greater sin.' *And from thenceforth Pilate sought to release him: but the Jews cried out, saying, 'If thou let this man go, thou art not Caesar's friend: whosoever maketh himself a king speaketh against Caesar.' When Pilate therefore heard that saying, he brought Jesus forth, and sat down in the judgment seat in a place that is called the Pavement, but in the Hebrew, Gabbatha. And it was the preparation of the Passover, and about the sixth hour: and he saith unto the Jews, 'Behold your King!' But they cried out, 'Away with him, away with him, crucify him.' Pilate saith unto them, 'Shall I crucify your King?' The chief priest answered, 'We have no king but Caesar.' Then delivered he him therefore unto them to be crucified. And they took Jesus, and led him away. And he bearing his cross went forth into a place called the place of a skull, which is called in the Hebrew, Golgotha: Where they crucified him, and two other with him, on either side one, and Jesus in the midst. And Pilate wrote a title, and put it on the cross. And the writing was, JESUS OF NAZARETH THE KING OF THE JEWS. This title then read many of the Jews: for the place where Jesus was crucified was nigh to the city: and it was written in Hebrew, and Greek, and Latin. Then said the chief priests of the Jews to Pilate, 'Write not, The King of the Jews; but that he said, "I am King of the Jews."' Pilate answered, 'What I have written I have written'"* (John 19:7-22).

From the words of Jesus spoken to Pontius Pilate, the Roman prefect over Judea, we learn that Jesus was born to be a king to proclaim the truth. But we also learn that his kingdom was not of the world (i.e., the world of the Roman Empire that was influenced by Satan's selfish, greedy ways). Pilate responded, "What is truth?"

We also learn from Jesus's words that Pilate would have had no power over Jesus had it not been given to him from God above.

This whole encounter with Jesus and his Jewish accusers greatly frightened Pontius Pilate even though he represented what many men thought was the most powerful government on earth at that time.

So putting this altogether, what does it all mean and what is the truth that Jesus said he was born to proclaim?

It should be clear from everything recorded here and in other scripture that Jesus said and did the truth. Actually, he is the very embodiment of the *truth* that he proclaimed because the truth of the kingdom that he proclaimed is embodied in him as the king of God's kingdom.

Jesus proclaimed the eternal good news that he was sent to earth to proclaim. This good news was the truth that it was God's good pleasure to give his people (all human beings on earth) his kingdom and that this kingdom of God was literally *at hand! At hand* means *it is here!*

Jesus revealed that God's kingdom would be manifested in the hearts of mankind as a grain of mustard seed and that God would empower this seed to overcome and completely take over the kingdoms of the world that are dominated by Satan and his evil influences (viruses). This is how God is restoring his kingdom ways and means on earth.

I believe God's righteous kingdom is the ultimate new world order that the so-called New Age movement and all the conspiracy theorists are all talking about. It is the global rule of God's law and order on earth. It replaces the old world order that has been influenced and corrupted by Satan. This corrupted world order is metaphorically represented in biblical prophecy as Babylon the Great.

Satan has deceived many today to believe the lie that the United States of America is the very essence of Babylon the

Great. Satan blinds these people to the fact that America was founded upon and continues to operate on the rule of law and order of God's righteous kingdom!

It is not surprising that these blinded people can only see the evil works that Satan has wrought in American government, commerce, and society. But they are unable to see how Jesus is destroying these evil works *through* the good offices of the government of the United States of America.

When our government's police and watchdog agencies such as the FBI, ATF, US Marshals, and local sheriffs and police forces expose corruption in the business world as with Enron, MCI, and Adelphia Cable, this is the righteous hand of God working through the US Government to be a terror to evil works as per Romans 13:1-3.

Likewise, when corruption with members of congress is exposed, as with the bribery case of Representative Randy "Duke" Cunningham, this is also the hand of God at work and is the fulfillment of Jesus's prophetic word that everything hidden in darkness will be exposed to the light of truth (see Luke 12:2).

When we see a congressional bill labeled the Jubilee Act, we see God's laws of debt relief reflected. (Note: The Jubilee Act, S 2166, never became law.)

If America's government were as thoroughly corrupt as the whore of Babylon is depicted in the book of Revelation, then it would not be in the business of exposing evil. Instead it would be concealing evil and sweeping it under the rug.

There is good reason why our government exposes evil and does not usually seek to conceal it. It is because all Americans as well as all human beings are created in the image of God (the DNA of Christ), and therefore, we, as the children of God, hunger and thirst after the righteousness of our heavenly Father, and we cannot tolerate unrighteousness in our community life for very long.

I have noticed when my church group sings at prisons that many hardened criminals are attracted to Jesus and his cross. They love to sing about clinging to his old rugged cross.

When Jesus spoke of the judgment of Satan's unrighteous world, he also prophesied that if he was lifted up (on the cross), he would draw all men unto himself. I believe these words of Jesus have a way of melting the coldest of hearts because most all men know who Jesus is and know for sure in their heart of hearts that with Jesus everything is going to be OK.

In the popular and delightfully humorous TV sitcom *Everybody Loves Raymond*, Ray Milano plays an innocent, childlike man who always means well, but through his childlike ignorance, he does not always seem to do well.

In the actual sitcom of our lives, Jesus Christ not only means well, he always does well so that everything always works out for our good in the end. An appropriate title for this real-life sitcom might be *Everybody Loves Jesus*.

I think the fact that so many millions of people throughout the world actually do "love Jesus" is the reason why so many millions flocked to see Mel Gibson's movie *The Passion of the Christ*, and they were deeply moved by it. I was particularly moved by seeing the Roman centurion look up to Jesus hanging on the cross and exclaim, "Surely, this is the Son of God!"

When I came out of the movie theater, the reality hit me that this was not just a movie.

Jesus's passion that was so vividly depicted actually happened, and three days later, he rose from the grave, and he is alive today and forevermore completely engaged in completing the work of his Father and our Father to restore his righteous kingdom on planet earth.

And I know and I can clearly see spiritually that he is very much at work in the minds and hearts of most all Americans to make our nation truly one nation under the God in whom we all trust, whether we profess to be Christians, Jews, Muslims, Hindus, Buddhists, or whatever.

I ignore those who are concerned that the all-seeing eye atop the unfinished pyramid on our dollar bill is an evil cult symbol associated with the underworld religion of Egypt or with the Masonic order. The truth is that there is only one God who sees all things he has created, and he is pleased with what he sees. It does not matter what symbols, artworks, or other expressions are used by what religions, cultures, or secret groups to represent the all-seeing, all-knowing living God just as long as he alone is worshipped and praised instead of dumb idols that neither think nor speak.

America will always be one nation under God. But as with all nations, we have been a work in progress in transition from the kingdoms of the world into the kingdom of God and of his Christ.

God's ways are supplanting the selfish ways of the devil that have been hindering the progress of all mankind to enjoy the righteous, abundant life of God's kingdom on earth. But much progress has been made toward this end. It is what many call the progress of civilization. But from many men's viewpoints, this progress has come about through the hand of man and not through the hand of God. But the truth is, all along the way, God has directed our steps as per God's word that says, *"Man devises his way in his heart but the Lord directs his steps"* (see Proverbs 16:9).

Those who are spiritual can clearly see God's kingdom's light at the end of the tunnel because we are very near and fast approaching the end of the age of sin and evil. The zeal of the Lord is performing this.

Those with spiritually mature eyes understand these things, and they can see how much prophecy has already been fulfilled: We know that Jesus Christ came to earth at the time appointed in prophecy, and he was taken up to heaven until the times of the restitution of all things as St. Peter testified just after he and St. John healed the man that was lame from his birth. St. Peter addressed the crowd, saying,

> ¹² *"Ye men of Israel, why marvel ye at this? or why look ye so earnestly on us, as though by our own power or holiness we had made this man to walk?*
>
> ¹³ *"The God of Abraham, and of Isaac, and of Jacob, the God of our fathers, hath glorified his Son Jesus; whom ye delivered up, and denied him in the presence of Pilate, when he was determined to let him go.*
>
> ¹⁴ *"But ye denied the Holy One and the Just, and desired a murderer to be granted unto you;*
>
> ¹⁵ *"And killed the Prince of life, whom God hath raised from the dead; whereof we are witnesses.*
>
> ¹⁶ *"And his name through faith in his name hath made this man strong, whom ye see and know: yea, the faith which is by him hath given him this perfect soundness in the presence of you all.*
>
> ¹⁷ *"And now, brethren, I wot that through ignorance ye did it, as did also your rulers.*
>
> ¹⁸ *"But those things, which God before had shewed by the mouth of all his prophets, that Christ should suffer, he hath so fulfilled.*
>
> ¹⁹ *"Repent ye therefore, and be converted, that your sins may be blotted out, when the times of refreshing shall come from the presence of the Lord;*
>
> ²⁰ *"And he shall send Jesus Christ, which before was preached unto you:*
>
> ²¹ *"Whom the heaven must receive until the times of restitution of all things, which God hath spoken by the mouth of all his holy prophets since the world began.*
>
> ²² *"For Moses truly said unto the fathers, 'A prophet shall the Lord your God raise up unto you of your brethren,*

like unto me; him shall ye hear in all things whatsoever he shall say unto you.'

[23] *"And it shall come to pass, that every soul, which will not hear that prophet, shall be destroyed from among the people."*

For the past two thousand years, Jesus has been with the Father in heaven, spiritually preparing for the restitution of all things.

And Jesus is about to return to earth in his glorified bodily form as depicted in Revelation 19. The restitution of all things begins with the exposure of all evils and iniquities so that all sin may end and all iniquities may be reconciled in accordance with Daniel 9:24.

The current economic crisis in the world has all happened according to God's master kingdom plan in which iniquity will gradually progress until it reaches its fullness so it can then be exposed and eradicated and reconciled.

For example, the iniquities in the mortgage market reached its fullness a few years ago, and now much of the fraudulent lending practices have been exposed so that foreclosure judges are now no longer deceived by attorneys who represent foreclosing lenders. The iniquities of the mortgage market will now be reconciled with God's righteous jubilee lending laws that will not permit a man to lose his home through foreclosure. God's laws against usury will again be applied as they were in ancient Israel to put an end to the current usurious lending practices that enslave debtors.

This is but the tip of the iceberg with respect to how all iniquities will be reconciled though the full implementation of God's kingdom ways and means. According to prophecy, Messiah Jesus first came to proclaim liberty to the captives (slaves) to set them free. Then he proclaimed the day of vengeance of our God; to comfort all who mourn (see Isaiah 61:1-2). We are now in the day of vengeance of our God.

God's Kingdom Ways and Means

The US Congressional Committee of Ways and Means is a government body that is charged with reviewing and making recommendations for government budgets. The term "ways and means" originated with the English Parliament (later the British Parliament and UK Parliament) and refers to the provision of revenue to meet national expenditure requirements and to forward the objectives of economic policy. Ways and means are principally provided by the imposition of taxation.

In this chapter, "kingdom ways and means" refers to the ways and means God employs to administer his kingdom on earth. In his master plan for earth, God has created man and his governments to administer God's kingdom on earth through the application of his ways and means through the governments of mankind.

In his unfathomable wisdom, God has created an influence called Satan or the devil to try to test, tempt, and influence mankind to twist God's righteous ways and means to administer a counterfeit evil kingdom that operates in opposition to God's kingdom on earth. God has ordained that as mankind experiences the evil end results (consequences) of twisting God's ways and means for mankind's selfish ends and purposes apart from God, mankind will eventually learn how to properly rule on earth in the goodness and perfection of God's kingdom ways and means.

In other words, God teaches mankind how to make good decisions by allowing him to make bad decisions and to experience the bad consequences of those bad decisions.

In actuality, God uses the influences of Satan to train and spiritually perfect (mature) mankind to be conformed into the fullness of the image and stature of God (Christ). This image of God was fully manifested in the man Christ Jesus who, during his life on earth, never succumbed to the temptations of Satan to twist God's ways and means for selfish ends. When Satan tempted Jesus in the wilderness for forty days, he was trying to get Jesus to bow to his throne of self-emulation and self-aggrandizement that actually reigns in the hearts of most all mankind to some degree. But Jesus would not bow to Satan because he knew in his heart that all mankind, including Satan and his fallen angels, would eventually bow to him for the glory of God, the Father of all righteousness. Jesus knew in his heart that the kingdoms Satan offered to him were his already. That is why he responded to Satan, "It is written, thou shalt not tempt the Lord thy God."

Some as they read this book may be tempted by Satan to think that it was easy for the man Christ Jesus to resist the temptations of Satan because he was the only begotten Son of God. But this is not true. Jesus learned to obey God as he denied himself and suffered with great agony, finally giving up his earthly life on the cross of Calvary. In so doing, Jesus demonstrated to all mankind that we also must and will deny ourselves so we too will learn to obey God to do his will instead of ours.

As Jesus hung bleeding and dying on the cross, he further demonstrated God's way of forgiveness, saying, "Lord, forgive them for they know not what they do."

When Jesus said his kingdom was not of this world, he did not mean it was not on earth. His whole ministry was to proclaim that the kingdom of God is at hand on earth. Jesus came to earth to replace the evil kingdoms of this world with the righteous kingdom of God.

"My Ways Are Not Your Ways," Saith the Lord

Here are some of the ways and means of the Lord.

All these ways and means of God's kingdom work together for our good.

The Ways of Heaven: When Jesus taught us to pray, "Thy kingdom come, thy will be done on earth as it is in heaven," he was praying that the ways of heaven would become the ways of God's creation on earth.

The Way, the Truth, and the Life: Jesus said he is the way, the truth, and the life. No man comes to the Father but through him. But no man comes to Jesus unless the father draws him. And when God removes the devil and his tares, the draw of God is irresistible. Then the sons of God (the wheat) will shine like the sun in his holy kingdom on earth.

The Way of Relationships: God's kingdom ways and means are designed to operate through harmonious, loving relationships between all human beings and God. Jesus prayed that we would all be *one* even as he was *one* with his and our heavenly Father. In God's transitional kingdom, "No man is an island. No man stands alone. Each man's joy is our joy. Each man's grief is our own" (words modified from Joan Baez).

In God's restored and completed kingdom, there will be no more grief or sorrow, no more war, no more death or dying—only righteousness, peace, and joy in all relationships on earth.

The Narrow Way to the Kingdom: Jesus said wide is the road to destruction, but narrow is the path to life in God's kingdom. The prophet Isaiah declares, *"All we like sheep have gone astray; we have turned everyone to his own way; and the Lord hath laid on him the iniquity of us all"* (Isaiah 53:6).

As our good shepherd, Jesus came to earth to take us back to the path of God's kingdom of righteousness, peace, and joy in the Holy Spirit.

Jesus said, "Now is the judgment of this world. Now is the prince of this world cast out. And I, if I be lifted up, I will draw all men unto me." With the devil cast out, no one will try or even want to resist the draw of Jesus. Therefore all mankind will be saved.

The Way of Righteousness (Holiness): The Bible reveals that all human beings were created in the image of Christ who is holy and righteous. Therefore we all have the potential to be holy and righteous just like Jesus. We need only to understand this and to learn to walk in this righteousness. We cannot strive to be righteous or to attain righteousness in our selfish self by anything we may do, say, or believe because the seed of selfishness cannot be righteous because it was created by God to be unrighteous. Unrighteousness is the nature of the satanic seed in mankind. As God matures and renews our spiritual minds, we are gradually able to distinguish the difference between the satanic seed (or virus) tempting (influencing) us to do unrighteous things and the influence of God's righteous seed directing us to do righteous things. As we spiritually mature to think and operate with the mind of Christ, we are then able to choose to follow God's righteous ways and to reject the selfish ways of the devil. This is the sovereign work of God that transforms us into the fullness of the character and stature of Christ.

In Sigmund Freud's complex theories of personality, which set the groundwork for modern psychology, he seems to recognize and distinguish our selfish satanic self from our godly righteous self. In Freud's theories, it seems to me he used the terms *id* and *ego* to label the selfish satanic self. And he used the term *superego* to label the godly self in each human being. St. Paul calls the godly, unselfish man the inward man that delights in the law of God. Paul called the satanic self the outer man. He also called it sin (see Romans 7:17-18). Paul said that our outer man is perishing while the inward man is renewed (matured) day by day (see 2 Corinthians 4:16).

Hindus call the godly self the higher consciousness or Brahman while the ungodly satanic man is called the lower self.

The Way of Peace: The Bible says the peace that God gives us passes our human understanding. In other words, it is a mystery to us. Yet we can still experience it. This peace is one of the main attributes of the kingdom of God that St. Paul says "*is in righteousness, peace and joy in the Holy Ghost*" (see Romans 14:17).

The peace of God is more than just the absence of war. People may experience the peace of God even during wartime.

The Way of Love: The Bible has a lot to say about God's way of love such as in the thirteenth chapter of 1 Corinthians and in the first epistle of John. But the best way to understand God's love is by experiencing it in our loving relationships with God and man. The love of God will constrain us to do the right thing.

The Way of Joy: This is also one of the spiritual attributes of God's kingdom. King David wrote that the joy of the Lord is our strength. King David danced for joy with all his might when the Ark of the Covenant was brought into Jerusalem. The tribe of Judah led the army of Israel into battle with singing, dancing, and playing musical instruments to express the joy of the Lord. This caused their enemies to freak out and become weakened so they were easily overcome.

The Way of Justice: A just weight and balance in commerce, debt relief, and righteous redistribution of God's wealth among mankind is a big part of God's way of justice. Jesus's work to expose and destroy the works of the devil is the very essence of God's way of justice.

God requires that mankind do justly, love mercy, and walk humbly with him, and he will empower man to do so.

The Way of Mercy: Mercy is forgiveness of debt owed. The debt (wages) of sin is death. But God's resurrection reverses death and gives us eternal life and thereby reflects the ultimate mercy of God. God empowers us to do justly, love mercy, and walk humbly with him.

The Way of Debt Forgiveness: Debt forgiveness is part of God's laws of jubilee. In US law, God's laws of debt forgiveness are reflected in bankruptcy statutes.

The Way of God's Judgment: God's judgment removes satanic influences (the tares or viruses of Satan) from the consciousness of mankind so mankind will be empowered to do the works of God. Jesus said, "Now is the judgment of this world. Now is the prince of this world cast out. And I, if I be lifted up, I will draw all men unto me."

The Way of the Cross: Dying to self, walking in unselfish humility with God and man.

The Way of Sharing: The flow and distribution of wealth throughout God's kingdom. John the Baptist said, "If you have two coats, give one to a person who does not have a coat." In the feeding of the five thousand and four thousand, Jesus did not have to materialize food out of thin air. Perhaps the little boy sharing his five loaves and two fishes prompted others to share the food they had brought with them. In the early church, the Holy Spirit directed those who had more than they needed to share with those in need. Also, the Holy Spirit prompted them all to consider nothing to be selfishly their own. With the early church, private ownership was considered to be stewardship, not selfish ownership. In God's kingdom, his unlimited wealth is shared by and through mankind. When people are greedy and hoard wealth, they impede the flow of God's blessings throughout his creation.

The Way of Honesty: When the tax collectors asked John the Baptist what they should do to do works meet for repentance with respect to following the ways and means of the kingdom of God, John told them to not collect more tax than what people owed. In other words, "Be honest."

The Way of Respect and Fair Treatment of All Mankind: When the soldiers asked John the Baptist what they should do to show they were following the ways and means of God's kingdom, he told them to do no violence to anyone. Here the word *violence* means to extort money by shaking and abusing a person. The soldiers were not to coerce people to give them under-the-table "protection" money to augment their salaries.

The Ways of the Times and Seasons of God: The fullness of God's times and seasons are prophesied and are sure to come, but for most people, it is a great mystery that will be revealed to all in these latter days in which we live.

The Way of the Word of God in Scripture: All scripture is profitable for doctrine, rebuke, correction, and instruction in righteousness so the man of God may be perfectly furnished unto all good works (2 Timothy 3:16-17).

The Way of Mystery: Those who are spiritually mature, like St. Paul, will be able to speak the wisdom of God in a mystery to make all men see what is the fellowship of the mystery that was hid in God before the world began.

The Way of Exhibiting Good Character: As God conforms us to the fullness of the image and stature of Christ, we will all exhibit the good character of Christ.

The Way of On-the-Job Training: This is God's way of training and perfecting humanity to be conformed to the image and stature of Christ Jesus.

The Way of Spiritual Warfare: God has ordained that during this present age or generation that spiritual warfare be waged in the hearts of all mankind for the purpose of maturing and perfecting all mankind to the fullness of the image and stature of Christ. This spiritual warfare has been mysteriously going on since the creation of mankind but is very soon to come to fullness or completion.

The Means of Grace, Faith, and Holy Spirit Empowerment: God gives us his grace and his faith, and he empowers us with his Holy Spirit to do the good works he has created us to do in

Christ Jesus (see Ephesians 2:8-10). Through the Holy Spirit, God imparts into the mind and heart of man certain knowledge and wisdom that empowers different men to build, invent, and create many wonderful things that greatly enhance our lives.

The Means of Prayer, Supplication, Intercession, and Giving of Thanks: Prayer is an ongoing two-way communication with God through which we come to understand what God wants us to do and why. It is through prayer that we walk with God and learn from him what it means to do justly and to have mercy. Supplication and intercession are specific communications with God regarding certain people that we are watching out for. In all things we do, we must always give thanks to God for all he has done for us. For without him, we cannot do anything worthwhile.

St. Paul wrote to Timothy, exhorting him to make prayers, supplications, intercessions, and giving of thanks for all men because it is God's will that all men will be saved and come to the knowledge of the truth.

If we fail to recognize the universal scope of God's salvation and operate in it, we may treat those of other religions and philosophies as enemies and hate them instead of love them as our brothers and sisters in Christ. Just because they may not agree with our knowledge of the truth and do not seem to even know Christ, that is no reason to hate them and to avoid any association with them. We must rely upon the words of Jesus to be true and effectual when he says, "Now is the judgment of this world. Now is the prince of this world [the devil] cast out. And I, if I be lifted up, I will draw all men unto me." We must never lose sight of the fact that Jesus is quite capable of drawing all men unto himself because all power and authority has been given to him. He is fully capable to save all men and to bring them to the knowledge of the truth that he reigns as king of God's kingdom on earth. It is therefore inevitable that every knee shall bow and every tongue shall confess that Jesus Christ is Lord to the glory of God the Father. Amen.

The Means of Taxation, Paying Tribute, or Tithing to Governments: God has ordained that all governments of men are to be terrors to evil works, to bring the vengeance of God upon Satan and his evil works, and to cast out Satan's influences from society and from the consciousness of mankind. When governments do what God has ordained them to do, they are worthy to collect taxes/tribute/tithes to carry out their God-ordained mission and purpose. But when governments use tax/tribute/tithe money for purposes other than for what God intended, then the citizens of that government are not obligated to pay those taxes/tribute/tithes to that government. I think this was the situation in the original thirteen English colonies in America. The colonists stopped paying taxes because they felt the English government was using the taxes they paid for purposes other than for what God intended. Their dictum was, "No taxation without representation." When pastors of modern churches that are not part of God-ordained governments teach their congregations to tithe to that church, it is a distortion and misapplication of the tithing principle.

The Means of Doing Good to Those Who Despitefully Use You: When people despitefully use you, they are under the influence of Satan. Satan's ordained mission is to get you to retaliate so there is constant strife and conflict. But when you, instead, do good to those who despitefully use you and instead of hating them you love them, Satan's mission is thwarted, and he departs and goes elsewhere, seeking others he may devour with his evil ways.

The Means of Sowing (Planting) Good Seed into Fertile Soil: The process of sowing and reaping (seedtime and harvest) has been established by God as a means to sustain our lives on earth so that we will always have enough to eat. When God allows disruption of seedtime and harvest through famine and pestilence such as what happened in the true story of Joseph in Egypt, God is training us to be good stewards of the land and to be good sharers of the increase and abundance that comes from good stewardship of the land.

The Means of Spiritual Protection: Our spiritual immune system—wearing the armor of God: the helmet of salvation, the breastplate of righteousness, the belt of truth, the boots of peace, and the sword of the spirit.

Socialism, Communism, Capitalism, and Democracy

During the 235 years of US history, our nation has suffered a bloody war for independence, a devastating Civil War, and two horrifying world wars.

In the twentieth century, we saw the rise of the German Third Reich, the Soviet Union, the Empire of Japan, and Communist Red China.

All of these huge, massive ventures were viewed by their instigators as New World Orders. But now we know these were all evil new world orders.

But only the German and Soviet ventures seemed bent on global domination while the Japanese Empire was initially conceived to be only a localized coprosperity sphere of nations of the Far East Pacific region under the domination of the Emperor of Japan who was believed by the Japanese to be a god descended from the sun. Amazingly, even educated Japanese were deceived into believing this lie. This would indicate that education does not keep people from getting mind viruses that cause them to believe lies.

Communist Red China was viewed by its main instigator, Mao Zedong, to be localized only within the borders of China.

Much has been written about the lives and thinking of socialist leaders like Adolf Hitler, Joseph Stalin, Mao Zedong, Karl Marx, and many others.

A common consensus says these men were all carnal and godless in their thinking. Even so, Hitler talked a lot about God. He was heavily influenced by Martin Luther's protestant and anti-Semitic thinking and also by the thinking of Roman Catholicism. He believed his national socialist party (the Nazis) brought about what was called the Third Reich as a revival of the first German Reich that is historically referred to as the Holy Roman Empire that Roman Catholicism believed was the kingdom of God on earth that replaced Israel as God's chosen people. This was a lie.

Mao Zedong must have also believed in God, judging by what he said to journalist Theodore White just before he died. He asked White how he thought the God of the universe would judge him for what he did to China.

Karl Marx, in his younger years, was an ardent believer and follower of Jesus Christ. His Jewish father was a convert to Christianity. Marx no doubt read the book of Acts's accounts of how the early Christians lived together in peace and harmony, sharing all things in common. He read that the wealthy among them sold houses and lands to redistribute their wealth to those in need. From this, he coined his famous mantra, "From each according to his ability to each according to his need."

Marx caught a vision of the socialism/communism that was inherent in the early Church's manifestation of the kingdom of God. As a social historian, he saw this as an inevitable outcome of mankind's social progress. He must have believed as I do that the kingdom of God is the ultimate new world order. But Marx may have failed to understand that only God can bring his kingdom to earth by changing selfish human hearts and minds to be more collective and unselfish in thought and deed. Mao tried to do this with his little red book, but he failed because it was not yet God's timing to change the hearts and minds of the Chinese people to convert them into the unselfish sons of God.

The early Plymouth and Jamestown colonies in British America tried at first to practice communal living where everyone worked for the good of the community instead of individual, selfish ends. But it did not work because it was of the flesh of man trying to force men to be collective and unselfish in their thinking. God was not in it.

Looking behind the scenes, spiritually minded men will see that Satan was the primary instigator of all these evil new world orders. Satan was able to operate like mind viruses in the minds and hearts of human beings like Adolf Hitler and Joseph Stalin who carried out Satan's evil mission to kill, maim, and destroy.

These so-called new world orders were actually smaller temporary manifestations of the old world order that Jesus referred to as hell.

Jesus knew and said that the kingdom of Satan is divided within itself, and therefore, it cannot stand (see Luke 11:17-18).

We know that Satan's kingdom is wracked with violence. His demons even fight amongst themselves, vying for power as was the case between Hitler and Stalin.

During the times of WW2, Satan's operatives joined themselves together in an evil coalition we called the Axis powers. But true to the divisive nature of Satan's kingdom, Hitler and Stalin's evil regimes did not trust each other, and they wound up fighting and destroying each other after they had both signed a nonaggression pact.

But Jesus said the kingdom of God suffers violence, and the violent take it by force.

What does he mean by this?

I would submit that he is referring to what Satan did to usurp control of the peaceful kingdom of God from mankind through cunning and deceit in the Garden of Eden. This caused the kingdom of God in the hearts and minds of Adam and Eve and their offspring to suffer violence. This violence is metaphorically depicted in scripture as the enmity God placed between the seed of the serpent and the seed of Eve. Satan's seed would bruise Eve's seed in his heel (i.e., in mankind's daily walk).

In spiritual actuality, there is only one God and one kingdom of God. The kingdom of hell is just a temporary usurpation of the kingdom of God. In this way, the kingdom of God suffers violence. But when the head of Satan's seed is bruised by Eve's seed, who is Christ, then the violence will be ended and peace will again prevail in God's kingdom on earth.

Metaphorically speaking, the keys of death and hell that Jesus took from Satan are the same as the keys of God's kingdom that he gave to his apostles.

Where Is the Kingdom of God Now?

The Jewish religious leaders of Jesus's day wanted to know more about the kingdom of God, so they asked Jesus, thinking that he might know if he was indeed the Messiah of Israel as he said he was.

They knew what scripture said about the kingdom of God, but they could not understand it because their minds were still carnal and underdeveloped spiritually.

Jesus spoke many parables about the kingdom of God, and he told them that the kingdom of God is within you. But they could not understand what he said just as scripture had long prophesied. Scripture said they would have eyes and ears, but they would not see and hear to understand (see Isaiah 6:9, Mark 4:12, Luke 8:10).

Everything about God and his kingdom would be a mystery to them. This is the way God planned it, and he had good purpose for planning it this way to keep Satan and his princes off guard, otherwise they would not have crucified Christ (see 1 Corinthians 2:6-8).

The Pharisee Nicodemus came to Jesus by night, desiring to see the kingdom of God. But before he could ask, Jesus read his mind and said, *"Except a man be born again, he cannot see the kingdom of God."* These words perplexed Nicodemus, and he responded, "How can a man be born when he is old? Can he enter the second time into his mother's womb and be born?"

Jesus chided his ignorance of spiritual things, saying, *"Are you a master in Israel and don't know these things? . . . If I have told you earthly things and you don't believe, how will you believe if I tell you heavenly* [spiritual] *things?"*

Many people throughout church history have read these words of Jesus and still do not know what he was talking about because their minds are still carnal and underdeveloped spiritually. This may be the case with many who try to read this book.

When people do not understand something like they think they should, they will often use their imaginations to concoct some incorrect meaning that is not of the knowledge of the truth.

Many people who are called scientists do this all the time. St. Paul said such people were ever learning but unable to come to the knowledge of the truth. Paul referred to their science as science falsely so called. But Paul warned Timothy to not waste time talking with such men because any talk with such carnally minded men would be just foolish babbling.

Now, back to the question at hand—where is the kingdom of God now?

The answer is the kingdom of God is in heaven where it has always been. But ever since heaven had come to earth in the material form of Jesus Christ as the son of man, the kingdom of God is now existing within the hearts of mankind where Jesus Christ has been living ever since the creation of mankind. Jesus Christ is the image of God and his kingdom in which all men are created. For as St. Paul wrote in Ephesians 2:10, we are all God's workmanship created in Christ Jesus unto good works.

But of course, most people who are still carnally minded cannot understand such things because they are spiritually discerned.

Most people have been taught to use their imaginations to understand the things of God that they don't understand. Or they have been taught to blindly accept the imaginative interpretations of their pastors and other men who are supposed to know more than them.

But the truth is that we have all gone astray, even our pastors. There is a way that seems right to man, but the ends thereof are the ways of death.

To be carnally minded is death, but to be spiritually minded is life and peace.

But we should not worry. Through St. Paul who received great revelation from the Holy Spirit of Jesus Christ himself, God has revealed that his will is to save all men and bring us all to the knowledge of the truth. Amen.

The lack of men's understanding of spiritual things is one of the greatest signs of the end-times. Jesus said the end-times would be like the days of Noah when men's imaginations were evil continually.

The disagreements men have today over what the Bible says is most astounding to me. But perhaps the most astounding thing is that men are so satisfied with their unique and diverse misunderstandings of what the Bible really says.

But when men come to the realization (and they will) that their doctrines and understanding of scripture is not of the knowledge of God, their hunger and thirst for righteousness and truth will cause them to seek God's kingdom and his righteousness just as Jesus said. And then they will know the truth, and the truth will set them free.

However, they will not find the truth because they sought it through their own free will or of the will of the flesh. They will find it only because God in them has driven them to find the truth according to his perfect will and purpose (see Philippians 2:13).

The Gradually Developing Righteous Attitudes of God's Kingdom Citizens

At present, God's kingdom citizens (all human beings) are all works in progress at various stages of spiritual growth and development. We are all in the process of gradually being conformed to the image and stature of Christ Jesus as the Holy Spirit empowers us to overcome the viral influence of the evil one in our minds and hearts. We all have mind viruses that must be neutralized by our spiritual immune systems that operate like how antivirus programs operate in computers. Our spiritual immune systems are metaphorically evidenced by our helmets of salvation, our breastplates of righteousness, our belts of truth, our shoes of the gospel of peace, and our swords of the spirit.

As this spiritual immune system activates, we will gradually learn to deny selfish attitudes and self-perspectives so we will come to the knowledge of the truth that selfishness separates us from the eternal life, love, respect, and trust of the one true and only omnipotent God, our Holy Righteous Father in heaven. And we will also learn that selfishness alienates us from other kingdom citizens, even from our own family members.

God, in his great mercy, will give us all renewed hearts and minds that will enable us to walk in his righteous statutes and to do them. And he will cause us to remember our past evil choices and the evil consequences of those choices (see Ezekiel 36:26-38).

We will no longer hold to the world's concept of personal ownership of anything because we will know that everything belongs to God. We will be grateful for whatever things God provides for us to use, and we will practice good stewardship of all these things, making sure nothing is ever lost or wasted.

We will be quick to share what we have with others as we are able (i.e., with others who have legitimate and righteous needs and who also practice good stewardship).

We will all eventually understand that God has designed us all to be conduits (vessels) of God's love and provision. When people hoard God's wealth and provision, they hinder the flow of God's blessings and prevent many from receiving his blessings. Those who do so may possibly suffer the same fate of Ananias and Sapphira who greedily held back from giving all they had promised to give from the sale of their properties. God struck them dead and removed them from the land of the living.

This struck fear into the hearts of all in the early kingdom community. But this fear was cast out as they experienced the perfect love of God working in their newly formed kingdom community.

We will be completely honest and righteous in everything we do.

We will all continue to have the attitudes and mindsets of little children who stand in awe and wonder, beholding all the beauty and glory of God that is manifested in his creation.

We will all know and appreciate the inestimable value of the love of God, and we will operate in it constantly as we continue to love one another.

We will all be poor in spirit, having no pride or desire to lord it over anyone. We will exercise our God-given dominion over God's creation as wise and righteous stewards, ensuring no one or nothing is ever abused or exploited in opposition to God's perfect will and purpose.

We will all have the attitude and mindset of the fictional character Uncle Remus in Disney's *Song of the South* who is at home in nature and maintains peace and harmony with all of God's creation. Like him, we might even have Mr. Bluebird on our shoulder, and we may even sing along with Uncle Remus, "Zippity doo da zippity-a, my oh my, what a beautiful day."

We will all hunger and thirst after righteousness as we were all created to do until the restitution of all things when everlasting righteousness fills the earth as prophesied by Daniel 9:24.

Though we may at times still act like children in the purity of our intentions and attitudes, we will have, for the most part, put away childish things that are unfruitful toward sustaining the righteousness and purity of God's kingdom on earth.

For the present, until the works of the devil are completely destroyed, Jesus will give us attitudes and mindsets of peacemakers (mediators) when there is a need to make and sustain peace and harmony in all of God's creation. But when Satan's works are all finally destroyed, we will all know and understand that the need for peacemakers will be diminished and no longer needed because God's kingdom of peace, joy, and righteousness will reign supreme throughout the earth.

The bottom line is that all citizens of God's kingdom will actually have and operate with the mind of Christ. We won't just try to act like we have the mind of Christ. We will actually have it in our inner man. And our outward man will have perished in the lake of fire. The mind of Jesus Christ and his Holy Spirit actually lives in us and directs our steps so that we always do and walk in the statutes of God.

God's kingdom citizens are all becoming pure in heart just like Jesus, which means we will all become completely innocent and free of all evil thoughts and deeds because through the cleansing work of Jesus's blood, God the Father has purged from us all motivations, temptations, or inclinations to sin against God, ourselves, his creations, or any of our brothers or sisters who we love so much. As we all become pure in heart, we all will be able to live in the immediate presence of God the Father and to see him face to face. The zeal of the Lord of Hosts will perform this. Amen.

All God' s Spirit Children will Inherit The Kingdom of God

In Father God' s master plan for earth all his spirit children will inherit the kingdom he has prepared for them. God' s first born son, Jesus Christ, said it is God' s good pleasure to give us (all mankind) his kingdom.

However, the flesh and blood of mankind cannot inherit or even see the kingdom of God because the kingdom of God is totally spiritual in righteousness, peace and joy in the Holy Spirit.

When Father God created Adam' s flesh and blood, he breathed his spirit into Adam and he became a living soul. The flesh and blood of Adam was created from the dust of the earth and is therefore earthy as St. Paul writes in 1Corinthians 15:45-58.

In these verses, St. Paul depicts the two natures of mankind. The first nature of man is earthy, carnal and mortal while the second nature of man is spiritual and immortal which is Jesus Christ, the Lord from heaven.

Moreover, the image of God in which all mankind were created IS Jesus Christ just as St. Paul says in Colossians 1:12-15,

> *Giving thanks unto the Father, which hath made us*
> *meet to be partakers of the inheritance of the saints in*
> *light: Who hath delivered us from the power of darkness,*

and hath translated [us] into the kingdom of his dear Son:
In whom we have redemption through his blood, [even]
the forgiveness of sins: Who is the image of the invisible
God, the firstborn of every creature.

Therefore, the spirit of Jesus Christ has been dwelling in every man ever since creation. St. John confirms this where he writes in John 1:4-9 that Jesus Christ is eternal life that lights every man that comes into this world. St. Paul calls the indwelling Christ in every man the mystery of Christ in you, the hope of glory. (See Colossians 1:27)

This truth has been most difficult for mankind to comprehend because Satan has twisted and distorted this truth in the mind's of men so they are unable to understand the truth of God that is contained in the Bible. But in God's good and perfect timing, all men will be saved from Satan's distortions and will come to the knowledge of this truth and all the truth of God.

When God breathes his spirit into mankind, his spirit has a round trip ticket, so to speak, so it will return to God according to God's spiritual travel plans for mankind. In God's plans, it is appointed unto men once to die and after that the judgment.

In God's judgment, the works done by human living souls on earth are judged to determine the works that were motivated by Satan and those that were motivated by God's spirit in mankind's flesh and blood lifetime. Satan and the works motivated by Satan will eventually be burned in the Lake of Fire that God prepared for that purpose while the works motivated by God will shout his glory forever in God's holy kingdom on earth.

The Bible says almighty Father God is a consuming fire but this holy fire consumes only the devil and his minions and their evil works. It does not consume God's spirit children whom he conceived in his mind before the earth was created. It burns away the evil in mankind characterized as wood, hay and stubble in 1Corinthians 3:12. But the works of God in mankind that are characterized as gold, silver and precious stones are purified so that the redeemed spirit children of God will shine like the sun in God' s holy kingdom on earth just as Jesus taught his disciples in his parable of the wheat and tares, as recorded in Matthew 13:43.

The Inheritance of God' s spiritual kingdom is a birthright that will be enjoyed by all mankind who were conceived in and therefore foreknown in the mind of God before the earth was created. God' s spiritual inheritance is not conditioned upon mankind' s willful performance and obedience i.e., whether a soul has done good or evil during his flesh and blood lifetime. It is conditioned solely upon the will of God to conceive mankind to be born into the world of flesh and blood and then to be born again into God' s spiritual kingdom according to his plan and purpose. Being born again means that Jesus Christ is formed in a man according to God' s plan that is stored in mankind' s spiritual DNA. This is what it means to be predestinated to be conformed to the image of Christ as per Romans 8:29. St. Paul refers to Christ being formed in a man in Galatians 4:19 where he says, " My little children, of whom I travail in birth again until Christ be formed in you."

Being born again does not come about through bloodline or by the will of man or the will of the flesh by accepting Christ as personal savior. It comes about solely by the will of God, when God conceived all men to be created and born on earth.

This truth is consistent with what St. John says in John 1:13: Those who received Jesus were all born of God, not of blood or of the will of the flesh or of the will of man.

But as a self-oriented Christian fundamentalist, like I used to be, I used to think that the Bible said that the will of man played a role in mankind' s salvation such as willfully accepting Jesus as one' s personal savior.

I also used think that when the Bible says all things work together for good to those who love God and are called according to his purpose that this set a condition that <u>only</u> for those who love God and are called of God will all things work together for their good.

But since God has renewed my mind and given me a renewed heart to believe God' s truth from his perspective, I now know that with God all things ultimately work together for good for all men whether they love God or not.

Christian fundamentalists place conditions upon most blessings that God freely gives to mankind without condition. Fundamentalists preach the unconditional love of God but they place upon it the condition that mankind must by an act of their own free will receive God' s love and accept Jesus as their personal savior in order to be saved and to receive God' s blessings. But the truth is God causes his blessings of rain to fall upon both the just and the unjust. And God may allow mankind to refuse his love in the temporal but not forever. Ezekiel 36:26-27 indicates that if a man' s heart is too hardened to receive the love of God, God will give that man a new heart.

Therefore in God' s glorious eternal plan, God' s love and salvation cannot ultimately be refused.

John Calvin recognized that to be saved, men must be called by God. But Calvin thought many men were not saved because they were not selected by God as God' s elect. He no doubt thought this way because the Bible said that many are called but few are chosen. And Calvin and his followers believe that those not chosen by God would be damned forever. Calvin failed to understand that the choosing of God was for his service not for salvation. All men are called by God according to God' s purpose whether it be for God' s service or for his own salvation. This is evident in Roman' s 8:29-30 that says, those who God foreknew, he also did predestinate to be conformed to the image of his Son. To be foreknown of God is equivalent to being pre-conceived by God. Certainly all men whom God has pre-conceived in his mind he also foreknows. And these verses go on to say that those

God foreknew (conceived) and predestinated he also called. And those he called he also justified and whom he justified he also glorified. Just because God does not choose someone to serve him in this temporal life does not mean that person will not be saved in the resurrection when God' s kingdom will be completed and fully restored on earth.

When God's kingdom is finally completed and restored on earth then there will no longer be evangelists telling men to "know the Lord" because then all will know him and gladly serve him. (See Jeremiah 31:34)

Most men who read the Bible may agree that all men are created in the image of God because the Bible says it very clearly three times in two Bible verses in Genesis 1:26-27. This means that men are spirits just like their heavenly father who conceived them all before the earth was created.

This being the truth, all men will therefore inherit the kingdom of God in accordance with God' s good will and pleasure. But, as St. Paul says we will all be changed from flesh and blood bodies that perish into spiritual bodies that cannot taste death. This will happen in the twinkling of an eye. St. Paul says our mortal bodies must put on immortality that is consistent with our spirits that have always been immortal because they come from God, the great immortal spirit that imparts eternal life to all mankind.

St. Paul says,

> "When this corruptible shall have put on incorruption, this mortal (our fleshy bodies) shall have put on immortality. Then shall be brought to pass the saying that is written, "Death is swallowed up in victory. O death, where is thy sting?" This truth is indicated in the Old Testament in the prophecy of Hosea in verses 13:14 and in Isaiah 25:9.

Hosea 13:14 says,

> *I will ransom them from the power of the grave; I will redeem them from death: O death, I will be thy plagues; O grave, I will be thy destruction: repentance shall be hid from mine eyes.*

And Isaiah 25:9 says,

> *He will swallow up death in victory; and the Lord GOD will wipe away tears from off all faces; and the rebuke of his people shall he take away from off all the earth: for the LORD hath spoken [it].*

The zeal of the Lord of Hosts will perform this. Amen.

David H. Thompson
West Palm Beach, FL
Phone: 561-313-5088
dthomp6161@aol.com
www.theultimatenewworldorder.com
www.thefellowshipofthemysteryofgod.com

www.ingramcontent.com/pod-product-compliance
Lightning Source LLC
Chambersburg PA
CBHW021241280526
45784CB00005B/2195

978 1 469 1 5 4 3 3 6